"Bill has been making me laugh for over 20 years! Bill is a terrific comedy writer. Now, he's come up with this great idea for a comedy book. Great fun! Very cool!"
— **Jay Leno**

"Bill Rodgers is part of the fabric of the Austin and national comedy community, from Esther's Follies to Jay Leno, and points in between. Bill has been making people laugh for over 25 years, and I'm sure his new series, *History Retweets Itself,* will tickle your funny bone. Damned clever!"
— **Jesse Sublett,** Author, Musician, Austin Character

"Bill has a fun way of turning a phrase. He kept me in stitches when he wrote for Esther's Follies. Bill knows where the funny is!"
— **Shannon Sedwick,** Esther's Follies

HISTORY RETWEETS ITSELF
TEXAS EDITION

BILL RODGERS

Copyright © 2016 by Bill Rodgers
All rights reserved, including the right of reproduction in whole or in part in any form.

This is a work of humor. Although reference is made to real persons and events, the dialogue, actions, and content are products of the author's imagination only.

Starpath Books, LLC
Austin, TX

Library of Congress Cataloging-in Publication
ISBN 978-1-944225-01-8
1. Texas—Fiction. 2. Wit and Humor—Fiction.
FIC Rod 2016
PN6149.R2 2016   813.54 Ro
                                        2015958357

Cover Design and Illustrations by Douglas Brown
Book Design by Danielle H. Acee

Manufactured in the United States of America
10 9 8 7 6 5 4 3 2 1

DEDICATION

*To Manning, the inspiration and love of my life.
And, to my brother Greg, with whom I've shared
years of laughter on the front porch.*

TABLE OF CONTENTS

PREFACE 1

CITIES & TOWNS 3

HEROES & BATTLES 53

POLITICIANS & LAWMAKERS 67

OUTLAWS & SCOFFLAWS 81

OIL & GAS 89

SPORTS & ENTERTAINMENT 99

ABOUT THE AUTHOR 112

PREFACE

This book is not certified to represent an accurate account of history. Do not rely on its contents if you are writing a doctoral thesis!

This is a look at historical events through the lens of modern day social media. It is not clear how tweets and hashtags can be generated by long-dead historical figures. The technology itself has offered these insights utilizing an enhanced matrix of hyperlinked search engine algorithms optimized across a parallel echo paradigm platform.

Or, it could just be a wild guess.

CITIES & TOWNS

HOUSTON

June 5, 1837

On this day...

the city of Houston was officially incorporated. It was named in honor of Sam Houston, the hero of San Jacinto, and designated as the temporary capital of Texas. At the time, there was reported widespread drunkenness, dueling, brawling, prostitution, and profanity.

And that was just the politicians.

#DontForgetSkullduggery

@SamHouston - OMG! I felt safer fighting the Mexican Army.

HOUSTON

June 24, 1871

On this day...

Houston's first public transportation enterprise, the Houston City Street Railway Company, was granted right-of-way for operations by the city council. The service originally consisted of mule-drawn streetcars.

Passengers said there was nothing quite like the experience of riding the streetcar on a hot afternoon behind an incontinent mule.

#DifferentKindOfExhaustFumes

#AndYouThinkYourTransitSystemStinks

HOUSTON

September 8, 1900

*O*n this day...

the Hurricane of 1900 made landfall in Galveston, 50 miles southeast of Houston. It devastated the island with sustained winds of 145 miles an hour.

The only other time the wind has blown that hard in the continental United States is during a Donald Trump campaign speech.

#SayItDontSprayIt

#TrumpsHairCanWithstandACategory5

HOUSTON

January 10, 1910

On this day...

voters approved a plan to dredge the Houston ship channel to a depth of 25 feet. Once completed, steamship service was established between New York City and Houston. In New York, Houston is pronounced "how-ston" instead of "hyoo-ston".

In Houston, New York is pronounced only when necessary.

#WePreferOurBigAppleBarbecued

#FuggetaboutitYall

HOUSTON

September 23, 1912

On this day...

Rice University (originally Rice Institute) officially began holding classes in Houston. This highly rated academic institute carries on many traditions. For example, the annual Beer Bike Race involves teams of students chugging 24-ounce cans of beer and racing a bike around the campus.

The winner receives CPR.

#ItsNotWhereYouStartItsWhereYouVomit

#MoreActionThanMarijuanaSkateboardRace

HOUSTON

March 7, 1927

On this day...

The University of Houston (originally Houston Junior College) held its first classes. It is now the third largest university in Texas. The school mascot is the Cougar, and the popular hand sign used by students is the Cougar Paw. Students form it by holding up their hands with the ring finger bent and tucked under the thumb.

Many UH students think of it as forming the UT "Hook 'em Horns" sign, then raising their middle finger.

#DontTryDoingThisInFrance
#NotAGoodSignToFlashInDaHood

HISTORY RETWEETS ITSELF: TEXAS EDITION, BILL RODGERS

HOUSTON

November 1, 1945

On this day...

the Texas Medical Center was officially established in Houston. It has grown to become the largest medical center in the world. The center includes 21 hospitals, eight specialty institutions, eight academic and research institutions, four medical schools, and six nursing schools. Over 25,000 babies are born at the Texas Medical Center every year.

That means more butts have been slapped there than at the NBA Semi-Finals.

#FullMoonHospitalGowns

#WarmJelloAndColdStethoscopes

HOUSTON

September 19, 1961

*O*n *this day...*

the Houston area was selected as the site for NASA's new Manned Spacecraft Center, now known as the Johnson Space Center. Astronauts train there for space travel in a huge pool containing 6 million gallons of water. They also train onboard a specially equipped jet aircraft, called the "vomit comet."

The nickname "vomit comet" has also been used in reference to a charter flight full of fashion models practicing their own method of achieving near-weightless conditions.

#HoustonWeHaveAYacker

#TheHurleyBirdSpecial

HOUSTON

April 9, 1965

On this day...

The Houston Astrodome officially opened, featuring an exhibition game between the Houston Astros and the New York Yankees. Being the first fully enclosed, air-conditioned domed stadium, it was referred to as the Eighth Wonder of the World. Other firsts associated with the Astrodome include the first animated scoreboard, and the first use of artificial turf, called AstroTurf.

The original version of AstroTurf has become outdated and is no longer used anywhere except on top of Kim Jong-un's head.

#HairClubForRuthlessDictators

#ILikedTheCompanySoMuchIShotTheOwner

HOUSTON

November 16, 1970

On this day...

The Galleria opened and has grown to be the largest fully enclosed, air-conditioned shopping mall in Texas. It was the first mall to have an inside ice skating rink. Many high-end boutiques can be found there, including Louis Vuitton, Gucci, Cartier, Armani, Chanel, Tiffany, Versace, and Prada. Overall, there is 2.4 million square feet of retail space containing more than 375 stores.

To put that into perspective, if you shopped at a different Galleria store every day for one year, you'd be broke.

#EnoughAlreadyWithTheShoeStores

#NeedAGPSToFindTheRestrooms

HOUSTON

August 30, 2012

On this day...

Reliant Stadium (now NRG Stadium) officially opened with a preseason NFL game between the Houston Texans and the Miami Dolphins. It was the first stadium in the NFL to have a retractable roof. Not only are NFL games played there, but the stadium also hosts the Houston Rodeo.

These are two very different sporting events. One features huge wild animals running loose across the field, jumping and bucking and grunting and snorting, trying to break free. And the other one is the rodeo.

#DontFeedTheLinebackers

#LassoAWideReceiver

DALLAS

February 14, 1855

On this day...

Texas was finally connected to the rest of the U.S. when a telegraph office was installed in Marshall, Texas, east of Dallas.

The Texas and Red River Telegraph Company promised city officials the installer would be there sometime between 1:00 P.M. and 1856.

@MarshallTX - Morse code for "bite me" is dahdididit-didit-dah-dit-dahdah-dit.

@MarshallTX– LMAO didahdidit-dahdah-didah-dahdahdah.

@Sting – dedododo-dedadada is all I want to say to you.

DALLAS

February 2, 1856

On this day...

Dallas was formally incorporated as a city, although it had been founded some years earlier by John Neely Bryan in 1841. Before European settlers arrived, the area was inhabited by the Native American Caddo people.

Although there are many theories as to specifically whom the city was named for, the exact origin of the name is not known, kind of like Lady Gaga.

@JohnNeelyBryan - It was down to two names. Either Dallas, or Funky Town. LMAO

@J_R_Ewing - My favorite town to be shot in.

DALLAS

February 25, 1888

On this day...

the Dallas Zoo officially opened in City Park, consisting of two deer, two mountain lions, a prairie dog, and a couple of eagles. Over time, the zoo increased in size and was relocated to Fair Park. In 1936, it moved to its current location in Marsalis Park. Each year, visitors thrill to witness the spectacle of wild animals being fed raw meat.

Kind of like watching the Dallas Cowboys defensive linemen eat during training camp.

#AvoidTheSnakePettingZoo
#MonkeysWillPhotoBombYourSelfie

DALLAS

May 19, 1894

On this day...

the original Parkland Hospital opened in a group of wood frame buildings at the corner of Maple and Oak Lawn Avenues. In 2015, the newest, state-of-the-art Parkland Memorial Hospital opened.

This new facility offers the latest in patient care technology, including the new iPoo digital bedpan from Apple.

#DownloadARingtone

#TheOtherBootyCall

DALLAS

September 10, 1907

On this day...

the original Neiman Marcus luxury department store opened in Dallas. Every year, they present their Christmas Book, which is a catalog offering unusual and extravagant gifts. It has included his and hers airplanes, and his and hers submarines. Each year, the items get more expensive.

This year, it's reported that the Neiman Marcus Christmas Book will include his and hers Nordstrom stores.

#ForThePersonWhoWantsMoreOfEverything

#ItsNotTheThoughtItsTheGiftThatCounts

DALLAS

February 28, 1909

*O*n this day...

The Praetorian Building, also known as Stone Place Tower, officially opened at the corner of Main and Stone Streets in Dallas. The 15-story office tower was the tallest building in Texas at the time, and considered to be the first skyscraper west of the Mississippi.

Of course, by most standards, calling a 15-story building a skyscraper is a bit of a stretch, kind of like calling the Cleveland Browns a professional football team.

#OrCallingParisHiltonASinger

#OrCallingRealityTVReality

DALLAS

October 19, 1917

On this day...

Love Field officially opened in Dallas. Later, in the late 1970's, it became headquarters for Southwest Airlines, the no-frills airline. Services offered on Southwest Airlines were very cheap.

For example, instead of emergency oxygen masks dropping down from the overhead panel, clothespins would dangle by a string to help passengers hold their breath.

#EmptyBeerCansAreYourFlotationDevice

#BungeeCordForASeatbealt

DALLAS

July 15, 1957

On this day...

the Dallas Market Center had its first event at the original building, the Dallas Homefurnishings Mart. Founded by real estate developer Trammell Crow, Dallas Market Center has grown to include four buildings totaling 5 million square feet of wholesale showroom space where manufacturers and industry professionals promote their products to qualified retail buyers.

To become a qualified retail buyer, you must show you have the proven ability to max out at least three major credit cards.

#ShopLikeItsSomeoneElsesMoney
#ShopTillYouDropThenShopFromTheFloor

DALLAS

April 2, 1978

O*n this day...*

the popular prime time TV soap opera, *Dallas*, first aired on CBS. It ran from 1978 through 1991, with a brief continuation of the series from 2012 through 2014. The story involved J. R. Ewing and other powerful businessmen who tried to out-cheat each other to get ahead.

Their motto: Keep your friends close, and their wives closer.

#RoleModelsForCongress

#YouScratchMyBackAndIllStabYours

DALLAS

August 13, 1983

On this day...

the Dallas Area Rapid Transit system (DART) was created to provide light rail service for commuters. DART passengers, on the whole, are known to be better behaved than passengers on a typical New York subway.

That could be because in Texas, many people are licensed to carry concealed handguns.

#TalkToTheGlock

#DontGoMessinWithSmithAndWesson

DALLAS

August 20, 1984

On this day...

the Republican National Convention opened at Reunion Arena in downtown Dallas. Over 2,000 party delegates unanimously nominated Ronald Reagan for re-election as their Presidential candidate. Typical of political conventions, party leaders negotiated party platform issues with a lot of behind-the-scenes maneuvering and deal-making.

There were more broken promises made than at a high school prom dance.

#FunnyHatsDontHelpYourCredibility

#SpeechesThatMakeInsomniacsDozeOff

FORT WORTH

June 6, 1849

On this day...

Fort Worth was established as an Army outpost on a bluff overlooking the Trinity River, named in honor of Major General William Jenkins Worth. It was located on what would become known as the Chisholm Trail where millions of cattle were driven north to market.

Since the streets of Fort Worth were filled with cattle, it's easy to understand why it was nicknamed "Cowtown" and not "Smells Like Flowers."

#WatchYourStepville

#FertilizerFLats

FORT WORTH

April 8, 1873

On this day...

W. P. Burts became the first elected Mayor of Fort Worth after the city incorporated. Located on the Chisholm Trail and the Texas and Pacific Railway, the Fort Worth Stockyards became a center for the cattle trade. Cowboys coming off the trail made their way to indulge in all manner of bad behavior at the saloons, gambling houses, dance halls, and brothels in an area known as Hell's Half Acre.

Or as it's now called, Spring Break.

@W_P_Burts - What happens in Hell's Half Acre will probably require ointment. LOL
#TwiceTheViceAtHalfThePrice

FORT WORTH

May 8, 1911

On this day...

officials of Texas Christian University held the cornerstone-laying ceremony for the first building at the school's current location in Fort Worth. Brothers Addison and Randolph Clark founded the Christian-based institution of higher education, which is affiliated with the Disciples of Christ.

And with all the beautiful stories in the Bible, TCU chose their mascot to be the horned frog.

@Addison_Clark - Hey...it could have been the TCU locusts.

@Randolph_Clark - Or the plague! LOL

FORT WORTH
January 12, 1961

*O*n *this day...*

the Amon Carter Museum of American Art opened in the Cultural District of Fort Worth. It houses an extensive collection of American art, including paintings by famous western artists Frederic Remington and Charles M. Russell.

There is something for everyone, except for those hoping to find paintings of longhorns playing poker.

#WhatAboutDogsPlayingPoker

#WhereIsTheVelvetElvis

#LetMeShowYouTheEgress

FORT WORTH

April 1, 1981

*O*n *this day...*

Billy Bob Barnett opened Billy Bob's Texas country and western nightclub in the Fort Worth Stockyards. It's called the World's Largest Honky Tonk, and includes several dance floors, musical stages, billiards tables, and in indoor rodeo arena featuring bull riding contests.

The hardest part about riding a bull in a honky tonk bar is not spilling your drink.

#EightSecondsToChug

@Billy_Bob - Good luck explaining how rodeo clown make-up got on your shirt! Yee haw! LMAO

FORT WORTH

April 26, 1991

*O*n *this day...*

the Bureau of Engraving and Printing opened its second facility, located in Fort Worth. Along with the original plant in Washington, DC, these two highly secure government facilities print all of the paper money for the U.S. Treasury Department. The materials and processes used in the printing of money are technically advanced.

For instance, the paper is scientifically designed to wrinkle and crease exactly to the point where the bills are rejected by the Coke machine in your company break room.

#ReallyRageAgainstTheMachine

#FortWorthMoneySmellsLikeBarbecueSauce

FORT WORTH

February 29, 1996

On this day...

the Texas Motor Speedway opened in far north Fort Worth. The 1.5 mile oval track hosts many auto racing events every year, including NASCAR and Indy Car races. The drivers are highly trained.

Even at speeds of 200 miles per hour, these cars are packed in closer one behind the other than college students in a Spring Break conga line.

@Jimmie_Johnson - My GPS keeps saying, "Please turn left. Please turn left. Please turn left." LMAO

@Jeff_Gordon - I've done more laps than a fifty-year-old stripper.

FORT WORTH

December 9, 2013

On this day...

American Airlines Group, Inc., was formed by the merger of AMR Corporation (the parent company of American Airlines) and US Airways Group (the parent company of US Airways). The merger resulted in the largest airline in the world, with over 6,700 flights every day.

Their extensive training center is also in Fort Worth, where baggage handlers practice "accidentally" opening suitcases so all the underwear comes flying out.

#SamsoniteManglersUnion

#FragileStickersAreJustAskingForIt

AUSTIN

December 27, 1839

On this day...

the city of Waterloo was incorporated. The name was soon changed to Austin, in honor of Stephen F. Austin, the "Father of Texas." The city became the official capital of the Republic of Texas, and later the state capital when Texas was admitted into the United States. Austin is also the county seat for Travis County.

Austin has so many politicians, stabbing someone in the back is only a misdemeanor.

#ArmTwistingBeginsWithAHandshake

#MudSlingingAsAFormOfFlattery

AUSTIN
October 4, 1876

On this day...

Texas A&M University (originally Agricultural and Mechanical College) opened at College Station, 100 miles east of Austin. This was the first public institution of higher education established in the state. Among their many traditions is the Aggie War Hymn. It begins with the lyrics, "Hullabaloo, Cancek! Caneck!" which, some say, according to legend, is the sound of a cannon being loaded or a train passing by.

Others say it sounds like the songwriter was drunk.

#BetterThanSisBoomBah
#ThingsYouCantSingWithAStraightFace

AUSTIN

September 15, 1883

On this day...

The University of Texas was established in Austin. It has over 50,000 undergraduate and graduate students, making it the fifth largest student population in the country.

Their school motto is, "Disciplina praesidium civitatis," which is Latin for, "Too hungover to go to class."

#NotThatTexasIsAPartySchool

#TheEyesOfTexasAreBloodshot

AUSTIN

April 2, 1888

On this day...

the Texas State Capitol Building was officially opened in downtown Austin. The state legislature convenes there on the second Tuesday in January of every odd-numbered year and remains in session for 140 days.

That's less than five months every other year, which doesn't give the lawmakers enough time to screw things up too badly.

#ImNotDoneBreakingMyCampaignPromises

#IWasJustGettingGoodAtTakingKickbacks

AUSTIN

April 4, 1910

*O*n this day...

the Congress Avenue Bridge officially opened. It is home to the world's largest urban bat colony. Every evening, people line the bridge to watch hundreds of thousands of bats fly out to feed. Now called the Ann W. Richards Congress Avenue Bridge, it crosses Town Lake, recently renamed Lady Bird Lake. The north end of the bridge intersects Water St., later renamed 1st St., and now called Cesar Chavez St.

With so many name changes, it's a wonder the bats can find their way home.

#CantReadTheStreetSigns

#CantAskSiri

AUSTIN

October 11, 1915

*O*n *this day...*

on this day, Austin's historic Paramount Theater opened as the Majestic Theater, on Congress Avenue. This ornately decorated theater was originally designed for live performances, although it was later adapted to show moving pictures. Many world-famous acts have performed there, including Harry Houdini, who, during his career, escaped from handcuffs, chains, straitjackets, and jail cells.

He was locked up more than Shia LeBouf.

@Harry_Houdini - Hey! Can someone get the childproof top of this aspirin bottle? LMAO
#NeverTriedDuctTape

HISTORY RETWEETS ITSELF: TEXAS EDITION, BILL RODGERS

AUSTIN

July 12, 1976

On this day...

the 17 remaining Moonlight Towers in Austin were listed on the National Register of Historic Places. These 165-foot-tall towers were first erected in 1894. Their purpose was to provide security by illuminating a circle of light in a 1,500 foot radius.

And they were effective, except for burglars and muggers who worked in a 1,600 foot radius.

#NotTheSameAsMooningTheTower
#PermanentlyHairyWerewolves

AUSTIN

September 20, 1980

On this day...

the original Whole Foods Market opened in Austin. The company expanded to include over 400 stores in the U.S., Canada, and the United Kingdom. The company's pledge is to sell only the highest quality natural and organic products available, which means their prices may be higher than other traditional grocery stores.

However, they do offer more upscale services to their shoppers. For instance, their shopping carts include a chauffeur.

#PersonalizedPersimmons

#MonogrammedPorkChops

AUSTIN

February 1, 1984

On this day...

computer giant Dell, Inc., was founded in Austin by Michael Dell. The company has grown to employ over 100,000 people worldwide. It began its operations building personal computers in Michael Dell's dorm room at the University of Texas.

Michael stood out among his fellow students because his was the only dorm room where the smoke coming out was from a soldering iron and not something that could give you the munchies.

#DontBogartThatSolderJoint

#AnAppleADayReallyPissesDellOff

HISTORY RETWEETS ITSELF: TEXAS EDITION, BILL RODGERS

SAN ANTONIO

June 13, 1691

On this day...

a group of Spanish Catholic explorers and missionaries arrived at a small Payaya Indian settlement in Central Texas. The Payaya called their village Yanaguana. The Spaniards named it San Antonio, in honor of Saint Anthony of Padua. Saint Anthony is the patron saint of finding things, even lost people.

That explains why none of the other saints like to play him at "Where's Waldo."

#YanaguanaSpurs

@Saint_Anthony - Two words: sofa cushions. Really. That's where your keys are. LOL

SAN ANTONIO

February 23, 1836

On this day...

Mexican General Santa Anna arrived at the Alamo with thousands of soldiers. They began to lay siege against the Texans defending the site. After 13 days, the Texans were defeated. The Alamo is considered the most significant landmark of the Texas Revolution, and is visited by 2.5 million people every year. Here's a tip: If you plan to visit the Alamo, don't make a fool of yourself and ask to see the basement. Everybody knows there isn't a basement in the Alamo.

Ask to see the attic.

#YouDidntHearItFromMe
#TellThemPeeWeeSentYou

SAN ANTONIO

March 2, 1910

On this day...

U.S. Army Lt. Benjamin D. Foulois made the first official military air flight in a Wright brothers plane at Fort Sam Houston in San Antonio.

Afterwards, Foulois was reported to say, "Dude, I must have gotten like three feet of air on that one!"

@Ben_Foulois - I feel the need, the need for a barf bag.

#JoinTheFiveFootHighClub

SAN ANTONIO

September 15, 1933

On this day...

Prohibition ended and minutes later, Pearl Brewery resumed operations in San Antonio, shipping out 100 trucks and 25 boxcars full of beer.

To put this into historical perspective, that's almost as much beer as is consumed at a fraternity kegger party.

#NoWorryTheHazMatTeamWillCleanThatUp

#DudeICantFeelMyFace

SAN ANTONIO

April 6, 1968

*O*n *this day...*

the HemisFair officially opened in San Antonio. The most prominent structure built for this World's Fair was the 750-foot tall Tower of the Americas.

From the observation deck, fair goers could clearly see their cars being broken into in the parking lo*t*.

#CarAlarmWasASurlyBulldog

#NoOne'sGonnaBotherYourVWBug

SAN ANTONIO

August 11, 1972

On this day...

San Antonio Mayor John Gatti declared August 11, 1972, "Cheech and Chong Day." The comedy duo performed a set to close out the festival held in their name.

After the partygoers left, cleanup crews had to get rid of more roaches than the Orkin man.

#SoldOutOfSnacksInTheFirstHour

@Chong - Hey, man, this Mountain Dew tastes funny.

@Cheech - That's not Mountain Dew, man, that's bong water.

SAN ANTONIO

March 14, 1992

On this day...

the Fiesta Texas theme park officially opened in San Antonio, located in what was previously a rock quarry. It is now known as Six Flags Fiesta Texas.

This park includes state-of-the-art thrill rides designed to spin, flip, fling, sling, twirl, whirl, and propel kids so they throw up all the expensive food their parents just bought for them on the midway.

#YouMustBeAtLeastThisTallToHurl

#YouCouldUseATicTac

SAN ANTONIO

May 15, 1993

On this day...

the Alamodome officially opened in San Antonio. It can be used for football, basketball, concerts, or conventions. The San Antonio Spurs played there from 1993 to 2002. The building holds 65,000 spectators and has 88 restrooms. That works out to one restroom for every 738 people. And chances are that at least one of those 738 people will try to flush something down the toilet that doesn't belong in a toilet.

That's why you never wear flip-flops to a ball game.

#ThingsASwifferWontFix
#PurellBetweenYourToes

SAN ANTONIO

October 1, 2010

O*n this day...*

the Joint Base San Antonio was formed by consolidating Fort Sam Houston, Randolph Air Force Base, and Lackland Air Force Base.

By combining these military operations, San Antonio is now better prepared in case there is another attack on the Alamo.

#FighterPilotsWithCoonskinFlightHelmets

#RememberTheAfterBurners

HEROES & BATTLES

HEROES & BATTLES

November 6, 1528

On this day...

shipwrecked Spanish explorer Alvar Nunez Cabeza de Vaca became the first European to set foot in Texas.

Being a forward thinking man, he immediately established the territory's first amusement park, "One Flag over Texas."

@Cabezadevaca - OMG! Visit our concession stand and try the suet on a stick.

#AdmissionIsOneChicken

#ButtSplintersOnTheWaterslide

HEROES & BATTLES

February 18, 1685

*O*n this day...

French explorer Rene-Robert Cavelier, Sieur de la Salle established Fort St. Louis at Matagorda Bay, which became the basis for France's claim to Texas.

Trying to fit in, la Salle invited the locals over for barbecued escargot.

@Bubba_la_Salle - Bon jour, y'all! Stuck the French flag in the ground and black oily stuff came oozing up. Maybe we should let the Spanish keep it! LOL

#CantSayMyNameInOneBreath

HEROES & BATTLES

January 3, 1823

On this day...

Stephen F. Austin was awarded a land grant from Mexico allowing him to settle 300 families in Texas.

Years later, Mexico would come to regret it, saying, "That wasn't a land grant. It was a vacation rental."

@StephenAustin - Well, finally. A nice, peaceful place to settle down. My BFF @GenSantaAnna seems to be an agreeable chap.

#SettlersWithWagonEnvy

HEROES & BATTLES

December 16, 1826

On this day...

Benjamin W. Edwards rode into Nacogdoches, an area under Mexican control. He declared himself Ruler of the Republic of Fredonia. A month later, when the Mexican army arrived, Edwards gave up and retreated from the territory.

His biggest regret? Not being ruler long enough to come up with a logo for Fredonia T-shirts and koozies.

@Benjamin_W_Edwards - Sorry. Did I say Ruler of Fredonia? I meant King of the Road. My bad.

#MexicoIsSoTouchyAboutTheirStuff

HEROES & BATTLES

October 2, 1835

On this day...

Texas settlers fought with Mexican soldiers in the Battle of Gonzales. This was the first battle in the Texas Revolution. The fight was over a cannon, which the Mexican authorities had given the settlers of Gonzales, but then wanted it back. In reply, the Texans fired the cannon at the Mexican soldiers.

Who could have seen that coming?

#LikeAskingComanchesForYourArrowsBack
#Doh

HEROES & BATTLES

January 5, 1836

On this day...

Davy Crockett arrived in Texas just before the Battle of the Alamo. He was known for wearing his signature coonskin cap.

It worked much better than his brother Pharell Crockett's armadillo cap.

@DavyCrockett - I'll be honest. Sometimes that old coonskin cap of mine could use a shot of Febreeze. Am I right? Whew! LMAO

#BeSureItsDeadBeforeYouPutItOnYourHead

HISTORY RETWEETS ITSELF: TEXAS EDITION, BILL RODGERS

HEROES & BATTLES

March 2, 1836

*O*n this day...

elected delegates led by David G. Burnet convened at Washington-on-the-Brazos, where they declared Texas' independence from Mexico. However, the declaration could not be signed by the delegates until the following day because mistakes were found in the document.

A little known fact: the corrections were made by Otto Spelzchek.

#WaysToPissOffMexico

#NowWhatAmIGonnaDoWithAllThesePesos

HEROES & BATTLES

March 6, 1836

On this day...

after 13 days of fighting the Mexican army, the outnumbered soldiers defending the Alamo were finally overwhelmed by General Santa Anna's forces. No prisoners were taken. A little more than one month later, a Texan army led by General Sam Houston would defeat General Santa Anna and his army in the Battle of San Jacinto.

#PaybacksAreHell

HEROES & BATTLES

April 21, 1836

On this day...

The Republic of Texas won its independence from Mexico at the Battle of San Jacinto. General Sam Houston led an army of Texas soldiers in a surprise attack against General Santa Anna's military, defeating them in just 18 minutes.

Turns out, the Mexican soldiers were more confused than Larry the Cable Guy trying to learn algebra.

@Sam_Houston - Charge! Wait...It's over already? Cease fire! WTH.

@Santa_Anna - Hey, we weren't ready! Do overs! Do overs!

HEROES & BATTLES

April 25, 1846

On this day...

Mexican soldiers ambushed and defeated American military forces led by Captain Seth B. Thornton along the Rio Grande. This was the beginning of the Mexican-American War. The incident was referred to as the Thornton Affair.

This is just one example of how an affair can go oh so wrong.

@SethBThornton - I tried to warn you, @Mexico, but nooooooooooo! Now you're no longer my BFF.

#DontPokeTheBear

HEROES & BATTLES

February 2, 1848

On this day...

the Treaty of Guadalupe Hidalgo was signed by the United States and Mexico. This ended the Mexican-American War and established the Rio Grande as the border. The U.S. purchased additional territory from Mexico for $15 million, including all or part of Arizona, California, Colorado, Nevada, New Mexico, and Utah.

It sounded like at good deal at the time, but that was before they knew California had smog, earthquakes, mudslides, wildfires, and Arnold Schwarzenegger.

#AllSalesAreFinal

#TheRioGrandeIsADysfunctionalBorder

HEROES & BATTLES

May 13, 1856

On this day...

Major Henry C. Wayne of the U.S. Army arrived at the port city of Powder Horn, Texas, on a ship carrying 33 camels. This was an experiment by the Army to use camels for transporting people and supplies across the Southwest.

The ill-tempered beasts were difficult to control, with more fighting, growling, spitting, and belching than the average fraternity party.

@Henry_C_Wayne - Sure, you can cook over burning camel dung, but you won't be very hungry.

#TheFlamingCamelDungDiet

POLITICIANS & LAWMAKERS

POLITICIANS & LAWMAKERS

August 25, 1829

On this day...

U.S. President Andrew Jackson made an offer to buy Texas, but the Mexican government turned him down.

The deal might have gone better for "Old Hickory" if his nickname was "Old Mesquite."

@AndrewJackson - Mexican officials are smart negotiators. They didn't bite when I offered to trade them New Jersey. LOL

#NotAGoodHaggler

POLITICIANS & LAWMAKERS

September 5, 1836

On this day...

former General of the Texas army Sam Houston was elected as the first President of the Republic of Texas. Previously, he had served as Governor of Tennessee. Once Texas became a state, Houston served twice as Governor, as well as its U.S. Senator.

Apparently, he could not keep a steady job.

@Sam_Houston - I've been in more positions than the Kama Sutra! LOL

#SammyGotGame

POLITICIANS & LAWMAKERS

December 29, 1845

On this day...

U.S. President James Polk signed a joint congressional resolution annexing Texas as the 28th state of the Union. Texas enjoyed the bragging rights of being the biggest state in the nation until 1959, when Alaska was awarded statehood.

Texas complained, accusing Alaska of using steroids.

@Alaska - We're twice as big as Texas. LMAO

@Texas - That's because all that blubber has gone to your butt. Maybe you should LYAO!

POLITICIANS & LAWMAKERS

January 20, 1891

On this day...

James Stephen Hogg took office as the 20th Governor of Texas. Hogg served two terms, and was known for his influence on the Texas Railroad Commission and anti-trust legislation. He was also known for naming his daughter Ima. Ima Hogg.

It was reported that Ima was eternally grateful her last name was not Hooker.

#ThanksALotDad

@Ima_Hogg - Stop making fun of my family. It's pointless to keep dragging us Hoggs through the mud.

HISTORY RETWEETS ITSELF: TEXAS EDITION, BILL RODGERS

POLITICIANS & LAWMAKERS

November 9, 1924

On this day...

Miriam "Ma" Ferguson became the first elected female governor of Texas. Her husband, James "Pa" Ferguson, had served as governor before her, but was impeached on charges of misapplication of funds, and forced to leave office.

This is just one more example of a wife showing her husband how to do something right. Or how to not get caught.

@Ma_Ferguson - Two governors for the price of one. That's not the same as buy one, get one free.

#ItsGoodToBeQueen

POLITICIANS & LAWMAKERS

May 1, 1937

On this day...

President Franklin D. Roosevelt arrived in Port Aransas for a fishing vacation, where he reportedly caught a large tarpon. He signed and dated one of the fish's scales, and claimed the fish was 5 feet long, weighing 77 pounds. In keeping with tradition, he hung the scale on the lobby wall of the reportedly haunted Tarpon Inn.

While many haunted hotels have their share of ghost stories, the Tarpon Inn is the only one where the ghosts tell fish stories.

#OooooooooooICaughtAWhopper

#IDidntOrderRoomServiceThatWasTheGhost

#HauntinentalBreakfastIncluded

POLITICIANS & LAWMAKERS

January 20, 1953

On this day...

Texas-born Dwight David "Ike" Eisenhower took office as the 34th President of the United States. Among the many accomplishments during his two-term presidency was his signing the bill authorizing the Interstate Highway System.

These are the highways that have been scientifically designed to provide rest stops at intervals that are 12 miles beyond the holding time of the average human bladder.

#EitherPullOverOrGiveMeYourCoffeeCup

#That32OuncePepsiHasToGoSomewhere

POLITICIANS & LAWMAKERS

November 22, 1963

On this day...

Vice President Lyndon B. Johnson was sworn in as the 36th President of the United States aboard Air Force One in Dallas after John F. Kennedy's assassination. Johnson was elected to another full term as President in 1964, with his famous campaign slogan, "All the way with LBJ." The same slogan was later adopted by Cleveland Cavaliers fans, hoping LeBron James would take them all the way to their first NBA national title.

Turns out, Johnson had more luck with it than the Cavaliers.

#WorkedForTheMiamiHeat
#BeatsDownInFlamesWithLeBronJames

POLITICIANS & LAWMAKERS

January 16, 1979

On this day...

William Perry "Bill" Clements took office as the 42nd Governor of Texas. Later, in 1987, Clements won the office again to become the 44th Governor. Soon afterward, he admitted his involvement with an SMU Board of Governors scandal in which he approved continued secret payments to certain SMU football players.

The school was shocked, SHOCKED that a politician could be involved in questionable contributions.

#MoreFunnyMoneyThanAMonopolyGame

#ItDontMeanAThingIfItAintGotChaChing

POLITICIANS & LAWMAKERS

January 20, 1989

On this day...

George Herbert Walker Bush was inaugurated as the 41st President of the United States. His famous campaign vow, "Read my lips: no new taxes," came back to haunt him two years later when he signed a bill raising income tax rates.

As a result, he lost his 1992 bid for re-election to Bill Clinton, because if anybody is known for honoring vows, it's Bill Clinton.

#ButIMeantItAtTheTime
#ItsNotMyFaultYouBelievedMe

HISTORY RETWEETS ITSELF: TEXAS EDITION, BILL RODGERS

POLITICIANS & LAWMAKERS

January 15, 1991

On this day...

Ann Richards was elected as the 45th Governor of Texas. She was only the second woman to hold the state's highest office. During her governorship, the Texas Lottery was instituted as a way to help with school financing.

In other words, school children were shown that, if you really want to achieve something important, gambling is a good way to do it.

#DoubleDownForCollege

#IveGotScratchOffCarpalTunnel

POLITICIANS & LAWMAKERS

November 7, 2000

On this day...

former Texas Governor George W. Bush won 29 states in the presidential election against his Democratic opponent, Al Gore. However, the results in Florida were so close, there was a recount, a Florida Supreme Court ruling, and a U.S. Supreme Court ruling before Bush was finally declared the winner by a narrow margin.

When Bush was told he won the electoral vote, he said, "I'd like to thank the electorals and all the other minorities who voted for me."

@Al_Gore - OMG! I can't believe he won. I'm so steamed, I'm melting the polar ice cap.

#ElectoralCollegeDropout

POLITICIANS & LAWMAKERS

May 12, 2003

On this day...

fifty-nine Democratic Texas state legislators went into hiding to prevent the Republican majority House of Representatives from passing a congressional redistricting bill favorable to the Republican Party.

While many Texas voters were upset by the tactic, others encouraged the rest of the legislators to leave, as well.

#CantScrewThingsUpIfTheyreNotAround

#GivesGerrymanderingABadName

OUTLAWS & SCOFFLAWS

OUTLAWS & SCOFFLAWS

July 21, 1878

On this day...

Texas outlaw Sam Bass, a notorious bank and train robber, died as a result of a shootout with law enforcement officials in Round Rock, Texas. Sadly enough, it happened to be his 27th birthday.

Even sadder, nobody sang "Happy Birthday" and wished him many more.

#WorstBirthdaySurpriseEver

@Sam_Bass - You really shouldn't have.

OUTLAWS & SCOFFLAWS

October 11, 1878

On this day...

outlaw gunfighter Bill Longley was hanged in Giddings, Texas, after being convicted of murder. He was buried in the town cemetery. Years later, Longley's father claimed his son had not died. He said the lawmen had been bribed to stage his hanging by using a rope trick, then whisking his body away, letting him escape to California.

Of course, they could have taken the bribe money and still hanged Longley anyway. What was he going to say?

@Bill_Longley - Hey, wait a minute! Where's my receipt? I'd like a receipt!

#NoNooseIsGoodNoose

OUTLAWS & SCOFFLAWS

May 23, 1894

On this day...

outlaw Bill Dalton and his gang robbed the First National Bank in Longview. One of the gang was shot and killed at the scene, while Dalton and the rest escaped with an estimated $2,000. When Dalton later used some of the $20 bank notes to buy supplies, authorities traced the money and tracked him down. Dalton pulled his pistol on the arresting lawmen and they shot Dalton dead.

It just goes to show that some storekeepers get really ticked off when you try to pay for things with large bills.

#DontEvenThinkAboutUsingTravelersChecks

#EnoughAlreadyWithTheCoupons

OUTLAWS & SCOFFLAWS

August 19, 1895

O*n this day...*

outlaw John Wesley Hardin, who once claimed he'd killed 42 men, was shot and killed by a constable in the Acme Saloon in El Paso, Texas. According to legend, Hardin once shot a man for snoring.

After that, Hardin didn't have much luck inviting his buddies for a sleepover.

@John_W_Hardin - Say what you want, but it did cure his snoring.

#SleepWalkersAreHarderToHit

OUTLAWS & SCOFFLAWS

May 23, 1934

On this day...

Texas outlaw couple Bonnie Parker and Clyde Barrow were killed by Texas and Louisiana law enforcement officials on a country road in Bienville Parish, Louisiana. During the ambush, the five lawmen emptied all of their firearms, shooting into the outlaws' car.

As a result of the gunfire, the car was filled with more holes than a truckload of donuts.

@Bonnie_Parker - I feel a draft.
@Clyde_Barrow - There goes the resale value.

OUTLAWS & SCOFFLAWS

May 25, 1962

On this day...

legendary Texas con man Billie Sol Estes appeared on the cover of Time magazine. He spent a lot of time in federal court and served a lot of time in federal prison. His swindles involved financing of non-existent fertilizer tanks, faked mortgages, and trumped-up cotton allotments.

He blew more smoke than Snoop Dogg.

@Billie_Sol_Estes - Don't hate the player, hate the game. Not that I admit there even is a game. Or a player, for that matter. And who said anything about hating? Not me.

#ScamBigOrGoHome

HISTORY RETWEETS ITSELF: TEXAS EDITION, BILL RODGERS

OUTLAWS & SCOFFLAWS

March 18, 2009

On this day...

Darrel Uselton and his uncle, Jack Uselton, of Houston, settled charges with the Securities and Exchange Commission, who claimed the two men conducted a massive e-mail spam campaign swindling investors out of millions of dollars. Their spam scam used so-called computer botnets to plant viruses in personal computers that would forward the deceptive e-mails throughout the Internet.

They almost succeeded in giving Internet sales promotions a bad name.

#WorksForMaleEnhancementDrugs

#IfItLastsMoreThanFourHoursYoureWelcome

OIL & GAS

OIL & GAS

July 25, 1543

On this day...

the first documented report of oil found in the New World was made by Spanish explorer Luis de Moscoso and his crew near the Sabine River on the Texas coast. They discovered a black pitch-like substance floating on the water and used it to seal the bottom of their boats.

They got an estimated 40 miles per gallon.

#YourMileageMayVary

@Luis_de_Moscoso - OMG! What a mess. This black oily goo is everywhere. Maybe we should put it in barrels and sell it to China! LMAO

OIL & GAS

September 12, 1866

On this day...

Lynne T. Barret drilled the first oil well in Texas, just outside Nacogdoches. The well came in at a depth of just 106 feet.

To put that into perspective, Tony Romo can throw a football 180 feet, often to a player on his own team.

@Lynne_T_Barret - One day, I was shootin' at some food, and up through the ground come a bubblin' crude. LOL

#ShallowerThanAKardashian

OIL & GAS

June 9, 1894

On this day...

oil was accidentally discovered in Corsicana by a company hired by the city to drill a water well.

City officials first became suspicious when they noticed their tap water burned brighter than the streetlights.

#YouveGotCrudeBetweenYourTeeth

#YourBreathSmellsLikeACrankcase

OIL & GAS

January 10, 1901

On this day...

a drilling rig at Spindletop struck oil, sending a gusher over 150 feet into the air and giving birth to the modern petroleum industry. The gusher continued to spew oil for nine days at a rate of 100,000 barrels a day.

Workers were ankle deep in oil - like walking across a Wal-Mart parking lot.

#OilierThanABucketOfKFC

#NotFingerLickinGood

OIL & GAS

May 23, 1923

On this day...

the Santa Rita No. 1 oil well came in with a gusher in the Permian Basin, convincing more wildcatters to explore the region. The well name was suggested by a group of New York Catholic women investors and their priest who blessed the well site. Santa Rita, or Saint Rita, is the patron saint of impossible causes.

An example of impossible causes? The Detroit Lions trying to make it into the Super Bowl.

@SaintRita - I just pray the Lions cover the spread! ROCL (Rolling on cloud laughing).

@SaintRita - PMHO (praying my halo off).

OIL & GAS

August 17, 1931

On this day...

Governor Ross Sterling ordered the Texas National Guard into East Texas to enforce the shutdown of all oil production there because operators had been producing so much oil, it was driving the price dangerously low. Because of such overproduction and price declines, numerous oil-related companies were forced out of business.

Thank God, that kind of thing couldn't happen now!

#OpecShmopec

#WillFrackForFood

OIL & GAS

August 3, 1942

On this day...

work began on a pipeline from Longview, Texas, to the East Coast in order to deliver crude oil to refineries there during World War II. Although it was 24 inches in diameter, the pipeline was named the Big Inch.

It was obviously named by a woman.

#SizeMatters

#LayingPipe

OIL & GAS

December 2, 2001

*O*n this day...

Houston-based energy giant Enron Corporation filed for Chapter 11 bankruptcy protection. The company's business reportedly collapsed due to upper management's deceptive accounting practices and failure to report unsuccessful deals and projects. As a result, Enron's shareholders lost $74 billion.

Even Bernie Madoff said, "Man, that's a lot of money."

#IfYouCantTrustAGiantConglomerate

#CookingTheBooksGetsYouBurned

SPORTS & ENTERTAINMENT

HISTORY RETWEETS ITSELF: TEXAS EDITION, BILL RODGERS

SPORTS & ENTERTAINMENT

October 26, 1886

On this day...

the Sate Fair of Texas opened its gates for the first time in Dallas. This annual event includes livestock exhibitions, music, art and history museums, the UT-OU football game, exciting rides on the Midway, and food. Lots of food. Especially fried food. You can eat all kinds of deep fried food, like deep fried butter, Oreos, Twinkies, beer, 'smores, and even a deep-fried peanut butter, jelly and banana sandwich.

Then, you can see just how good the fair's emergency medical technicians are.

#TurnYourHeadAndBarf

#DeepFriedRolaids

SPORTS & ENTERTAINMENT

October 18, 1954

On this day...

Texas Instruments introduced the first transistor radio in Dallas. The model TR-1 was portable and only picked up AM radio stations. It was about the size of a pack of cigarettes.

The reception was slightly better than a pack of cigarettes.

#LikeAniPodWithoutAllTheMusic

#ToShareTunesTurnUpTheVolume

SPORTS & ENTERTAINMENT

November 24, 1956

On this day...

the movie, *Giant,* opened across the country. It's a sprawling epic set in Texas, starring Elizabeth Taylor, Rock Hudson, and James Dean. To a large degree, the movie reinforced stereotypical views held by people around the world that Texas was filled with wealthy cattle ranchers constantly fighting with powerful oilmen.

This view was completely changed by the 1980's prime time TV soap opera, *Dallas,* showing Texas to be filled with people like J.R. Ewing, a wealthy rancher and oilman fighting with his own family.

#FatherCheatsBest

#OilInTheFamily

SPORTS & ENTERTAINMENT

April 13, 1958

On this day...

Texas pianist Harvey Lavan "Van" Cliburn, Jr., won the first Tchaikovsky International Piano Competition in Moscow at the height of the Cold War. Feeling proud of themselves for being the first in space, the Soviet Union had expected to boast their cultural superiority, as well, until Van Cliburn beat them in their own back yard.

The Russians were madder than Nakita Krushchev without a shoe to bang.

@Van_Cliburn - You've been schooled! LOL
#DropTheMic

SPORTS & ENTERTAINMENT

January 28, 1960

On this day...

the National Football League awarded a new expansion franchise for Dallas to Clint Murchison, Jr., and Bedford Wynne. The team was originally called the Dallas Rangers, but the name was soon changed to the Cowboys. Pro football was a lot different back in 1960, and the protective gear the players wore was inferior compared to today's standards.

For instance, helmets the players wore in 1960 were made from the same plastic as a Pez dispenser.

#CardboardShoulderPads

#BubbleGumMouthPieces

HISTORY RETWEETS ITSELF: TEXAS EDITION, BILL RODGERS

SPORTS & ENTERTAINMENT

September 11, 1960

On this day...

the Houston Oilers professional football team played its first game. The Oilers were a charter member of the American Football League, and were originally owned by Houston oilman Bud Adams. After support for the Oilers diminished, Adams moved the team to Nashville in 1997, where they were renamed the Tennessee Titans.

In other words, when things went bad, they just changed their name and moved to another town, like a bunch of mob informants.

#YouCanRunButYouCantPass

#MyJerseyHasAnUnlistedNumber

SPORTS & ENTERTAINMENT

October 24, 1971

On this day...

Texas Stadium opened in Irving, Texas, and was home to the Dallas Cowboys through 2008. The roof partially covered the stadium, leaving an open hole over the field. Cowboys fans said the hole in the roof was there so God could watch His favorite team play.

Now that the Cowboys play in their new $1.15 billion AT&T Stadium in Arlington, which has a retractable roof, God only gets to watch the Cowboys play when the weather is nice.

@God - Good thing I have satellite! LOL

@God - BTW, instead of OMG, I say OMM (Oh my Me). LOL

HISTORY RETWEETS ITSELF: TEXAS EDITION, BILL RODGERS

SPORTS & ENTERTAINMENT

July 4, 1973

On this day...

Texas musician Willie Nelson held his first annual 4th of July Picnic on the Hurlbut Ranch in Dripping Springs. The first several years of this musical event were attended by hoards of rowdy hippies and rednecks intoxicated on alcohol and drugs. Many of them were naked.

It was like Spring Break for adults.

#DontDrinkYellowBongWater
#DontLightYourJointOffASparkler

SPORTS & ENTERTAINMENT

May 1, 1980

On this day...

the Dallas Mavericks professional basketball team officially became a member of the NBA (National Basketball Association). In 2000, billionaire entrepreneur Mark Cuban bought the Mavericks for $285 million. In 2015, the team was reported to be worth an estimated $1.15 billion.

This goes to show that, if you want to quadruple your money in 15 years, all you have to do is become a billionaire and buy an NBA team.

#PullYourselfUpByYourGucciBootstraps

#MoreBounceForTheBuck

SPORTS & ENTERTAINMENT

March 13, 1987

On this day...

the first ever South by Southwest (SXSW) Music and Media conference began in Austin. That three-day event has now grown into an annual festival that lasts nearly three weeks, including music, film, and interactive conferences. At the 2007 SXSW conference, newly launched Twitter exploded onto the social media scene. The service allows subscribers to "tweet" messages of up to 140 characters, and now has 500 million users.

You can tweet and retweet messages, photos, selfies, videos and hashtags, or you can get a life.

##

#TweetLikeItMeansSomething

SPORTS & ENTERTAINMENT

March 21, 1994

*O*n this day...

actor Tommy Lee Jones won the Academy Award for Best Supporting Actor for his role as U.S. Marshal Samuel Gerard in *The Fugitive*. Tommy Lee was born and raised in Texas, where he owns two ranches.

In fact, Tommy Lee is so Texan, his pick-up truck has a bumper sticker that says, "My other car is a horse."

#ThatAintMudOnMyBoots
#ILoveTheSmellOfCattleInTheMorning

HISTORY RETWEETS ITSELF: TEXAS EDITION, BILL RODGERS

SPORTS & ENTERTAINMENT

August 22, 2007

On this day...

the Texas Rangers routed the Baltimore Orioles 30 - 3, scoring the most runs in a single game and setting an American League record.

In fact, the Rangers were so busy running bases, they didn't have time to touch themselves and spit.

#MoreRunsThanACheapPairOfPantyHose
#ScoreKeeperGotWritersCramp

ABOUT THE AUTHOR

When Bill was young, he tried to make his friends laugh and shoot milk out their noses. Now that he's older, he tries to make his friends laugh and shoot scotch out their noses.

Bill's comedy writing has taken many forms, including jokes, sitcom scripts, action-comedy screenplays, and short stageplays. He has written comedy sketches performed by Esther's Follies on Austin's famed 6th Street, and short plays performed by local theater groups.

Bill has written for Jay Leno for over twenty years. Bill's material has been used in Jay's monologues and comedy routines around the world.

www.bill-rodgers.com

www.ingramcontent.com/pod-product-compliance
Lightning Source LLC
Chambersburg PA
CBHW071523080526
44588CB00011B/1546